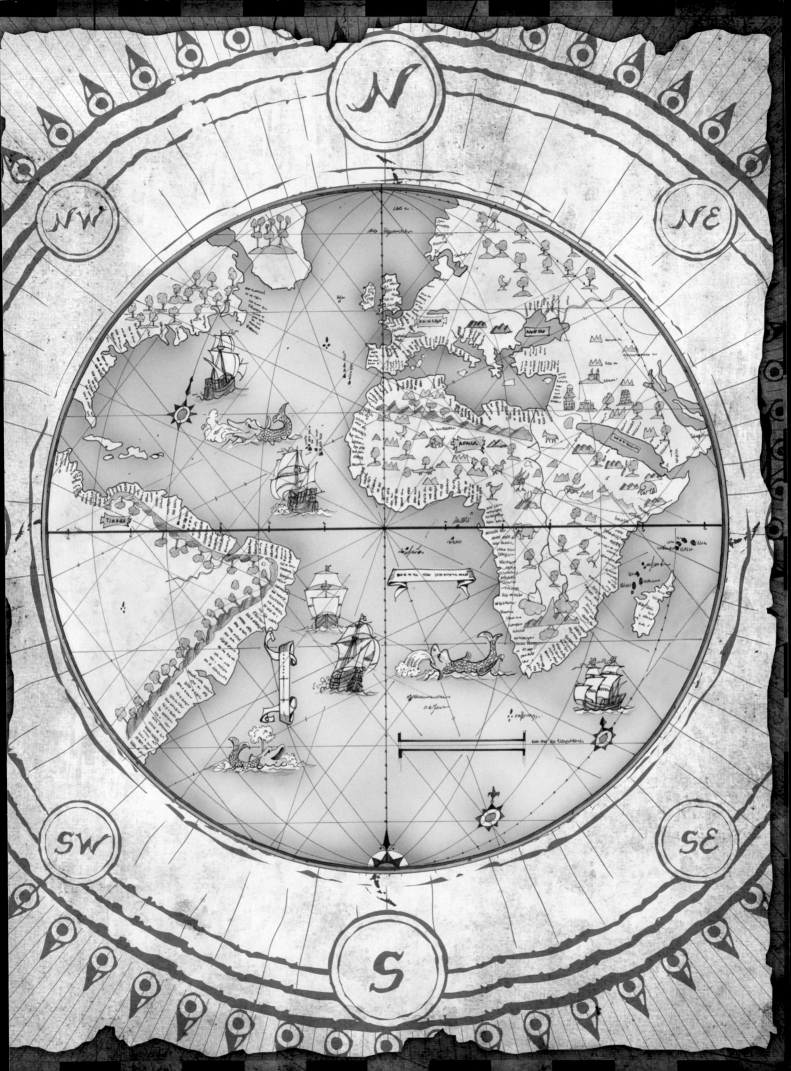

This edition first published in MMXVII by
Book House

Distributed by Black Rabbit Books
P.O. Box 3263
Mankato
Minnesota MN 56002

Cataloging-in-Publication Data is available
from the Library of Congress

Printed in the United States
At Corporate Graphics,
North Mankato, Minnesota

9 8 7 6 5 4 3 2 1

ISBN: 978-1-910706-90-9

EXPLORERS

The Story of
MAGELLAN

Jacqueline Morley David Antram

BOOK HOUSE

CONTENTS

INTRODUCTION

Ferdinand Magellan lived from 1480 to 1522. He spent most of his career as an army officer, living and fighting abroad, but he went on to become one of the greatest sailors of the 16th century. Magellan lived at a time when, throughout Europe, there was enormous interest in exploring far-away lands.

In 1511, Magellan made the voyage around Africa and across the Indian Ocean to the far-away Spice Islands (part of present-day Indonesia). He was the first European explorer to sail westward around America and reach the Pacific Ocean. He proved, beyond doubt, that the world was round, not flat.

He also discovered, to his dismay, that the route pioneered by earlier sailors, eastward around Africa to the rich Spice Islands, was shorter, quicker, and safer than the westward route he had set out to explore. Magellan did not live to complete his planned voyage around the world. He died far away from home, in a Pacific island war. But his voyage was continued by a professional sailor, Juan Sebastian del Cano, who brought Magellan's ship the *Vittoria* safely round the world and back to Spain. This epic voyage was the first-ever circumnavigation of the world.

A ROUTE TO THE EAST

Since 1418, Portuguese sailors had been exploring the west coast of Africa looking for gold, slaves, and a trade route to the east. They hoped to find a route around southern Africa. Many people thought ships sailing so far south would be burnt up by the sun or swept away by big waves. But in 1487-1488 Portuguese explorer Bartolomeu Dias sailed into the Indian Ocean.

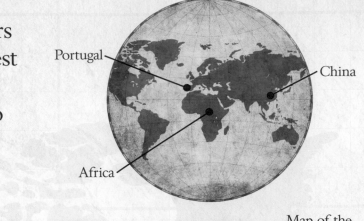

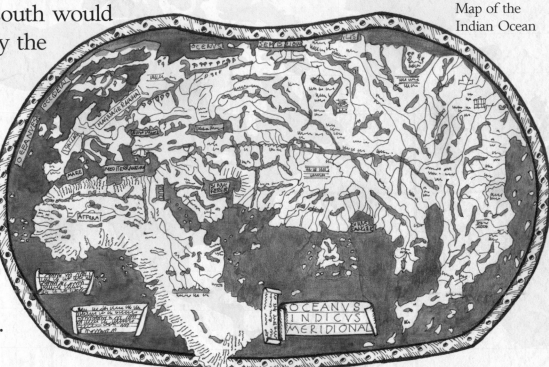

Map of the Indian Ocean

The Silk Road

The old Silk Road was a network of tracks that linked Europe and Asia. Goods were carried long distances overland on horseback and by camel caravans. There were trading posts along the way, too. Silk and fine porcelain were among the most highly-prized goods carried from China along the Silk Road.

For many centuries, both silk and porcelain were made by secret processes, unknown to Europeans.

SEEKING THE LAND OF RICHES

In 1492, Christopher Columbus set sail with three ships, hoping to reach the rich lands of Asia by sailing west. Instead, he arrived in the Americas, which soon became known to Europeans as the "New World."

Christopher Columbus claimed the "new" lands he explored for the King and Queen of Spain. Today, we know that Columbus had reached America, but when he died in 1506, he believed he had reached Japan.

Portuguese Explorers

Henry the Navigator of Portugal (1394-1460) funded many voyages by Portuguese explorers. He had a library of maps and travel books.

From 1487 to 1488, Portuguese explorer Dias sailed round the Cape of Good Hope and into the Indian Ocean. Vasco da Gama reached India in 1498.

SHIPBUILDING

To sailors strolling on the docks in Seville, Spain, the ship *Vittoria* (Victory) did not seem worth a second glance. Like other 16th-century ships, it was made of wood, with tough canvas sails. The *Vittoria* was old and sea-worn. Its timbers bore the scars of wild storms and many repairs. Yet ships like this were all Magellan could afford. He had bought five to take with him on his adventurous voyage. In spite of the *Vittoria*'s shabbiness and age, it was destined to win a place in history. It became the first ship to sail right around the world.

Spain

Carracks

Carracks were huge ships with big, square sails. They were designed to carry valuable cargo in their wide hulls. They went on long ocean voyages.

The *Vittoria*

A GUIDE TO BUILDING TECHNIQUES

Choosing and Transporting the Timber

Tough, slow-growing oak was the best timber for shipbuilding. Expert shipbuilders visited the forest to choose the most suitable trees to fell.

The leaves, twigs, and side branches were lopped off the felled trees, which were then transported to the shipyard.

At the Sawpits and the Workshop

The bark was removed and the trunks were cut into square sections at the sawpits. A two-handed saw was used—one man stood above, with the other in the pit below. Carpenters trimmed the sawn planks of wood into the shapes required using knives or a sharp tool called an adze. Planks for the ship's hull were curved into shape by steaming them over boiling water.

MAPS AND COMPASSES

For Magellan and his sailors, steering a ship was a matter of life and death. If they strayed from their planned course, they might run aground on sandbanks or be smashed to pieces on dangerous coastal rocks. They had only simple navigation equipment to help them and, in the early 16th century, very unreliable maps.

Once ships were out of sight of land, it was vital for sailors to know their exact position. If they got lost at sea they might never find dry land again. They would die as soon as their ship's supply of food and water ran out.

Spain

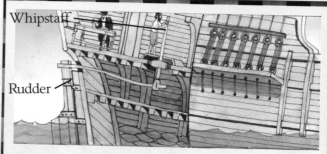

Whipstaff

Rudder

Keeping On Course

Ships were steered using a rudder—a huge underwater paddle at the stern (back of the ship). The rudder was connected to a long wooden lever, called a whipstaff, operated by a sailor.

Plotting a course

Navigation was fraught with difficulties. The exploration of unknown routes took great courage.

SAILING AND NAVIGATION

Sailors relied on the "Three Ls"—log-line, lead-line, and landmarks—to steer a course. But lead-lines and landmarks were only useful in shallow waters, or in sight of the coast. Other instruments were needed in deep waters.

Senior members of the ship's crew worked together to calculate the ship's course and steer along it accurately. They also kept a written record of where they had sailed in a diary, called a "log."

Navigation

Sailors used a variety of instruments for navigation. An astrolabe was a metal disc that measured the height of the sun above the horizon to work out latitude. An armillary sphere helped establish the ship's position from the stars. A magnetic compass aided steering and a sand-glass measured time.

Astrolabe

SABOTAGE AND SPIES

Ferdinand Magellan was born in 1480 in Porto, northern Portugal. He came from a minor noble family.

As a boy, Magellan served as a page at the royal court and went on to become a soldier. From 1511 to 1512, he served with the Portuguese army in Africa and the Far East.

In 1517, Magellan married Beatriz, the daughter of a wealthy Portuguese merchant. Beatriz's father, who traded in Spain, helped Magellan get an introduction to the Spanish court.

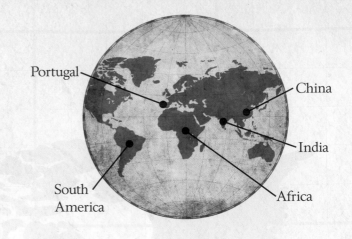

Portugal
China
India
South
America
Africa

Magellan with
King Charles

Magellan's Plan

By 1517, Magellan had a bold new plan to sail around the south of America and find a sea route to India and China. He asked Portugal's enemy, King Charles of Spain, to sponsor his voyage. Magellan may have quarreled with the Portuguese royal family. King Charles gave Magellan money to equip five ships based at the Spanish port of Seville. By 1519, they were ready to sail.

SAILING INTO THE UNKNOWN

King Manuel of Portugal sent spies to join Magellan's crew. He wanted to sabotage Magellan's voyage because it was backed by Portugal's ancient enemy, King Charles of Spain. King Manuel also tried to make sure that food supplies for the voyage were stale and moldy.

Ship's Supplies

The ships were loaded with flour and salt to make bread, and about 550 pounds (250 kilograms) of hard, dry, ship's biscuit—the sailor's basic rations. The ships were stocked with oak barrels full of fresh water, and 500 butts of wine. Magellan bought stocks of dried fish and meat preserved in brine (salt water). Around 6,000 pounds (2,700 kg) of salt pork were taken on the voyage.

THE ATLANTIC

Few 16th century sailors were willing to take part in a voyage into the unknown. So Magellan had to recruit his crew from desperate, disreputable men whom no one else would employ. He did not tell them his plans, so when they realized they were going around the world, they tried to mutiny and turn back. Magellan hanged the ringleaders and sailed on. Magellan did persuade a few well-trained sea-captains, like Juan Sebastian del Cano, to sail with him. Some young Spanish nobles also joined the voyage. They all hoped to make their fortunes in the Spice Islands.

South America

Magellan's route

Canary Islands

AFRICA

SOUTH AMERICA

Magellan Strait

Atlantic Ocean

The Southern Continent

Magellan was taking a great risk in trying to sail westward round the world. As this 16th-century map shows, many people thought that a vast, unknown southern continent would block his way.
His journey was not halted by the mysterious "southern continent." In fact, he found a narrow sea passage, leading from the Atlantic to the Pacific. Today, it is called the Magellan Strait.

CALMS, STORMS, AND MUTINY

Once through the strait, the water was calm, so Magellan called it the Pacific Ocean ("pacific" means "peaceful"). But soon they were in some of the world's stormiest waters.
Off the coast of Argentina, Magellan's ships were caught in a violent storm. One of them, the *Santiago*, was wrecked. Then the crew of the *San Antonio* deserted him and headed back to Spain along with most of the fleet's food supplies. The ships then got stuck in the doldrums—part of the south Atlantic Ocean where it is often calm. Without wind, the sailing ships could not move. Magellan's ships finally arrived off the coast of Brazil. The crew were tired and angry, so Magellan gave them a holiday on shore.

Creatures of the Deep

Magellan and his crew saw all kinds of sea creatures in the southern oceans. Although these all proved to be harmless, many of Magellan's sailors were still frightened of meeting the savage "monsters of the deep" described in earlier travelers' tales.

THE PACIFIC

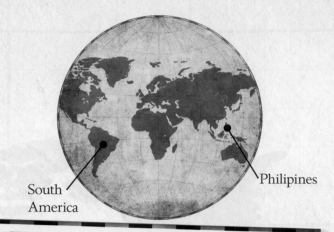

South America

Philipines

Magellan's fleet of three ships left South America heading north-west across the Pacific. They sailed for 3 months and 20 days without sighting land. The crew were filled with doom, fearing they would die of hunger and thirst. They ate anything they could find, including leather, sawdust, and insects. Mice were sold for half a ducat (a solid gold coin) each.

The Open Seas
At first, the crew were hopeful, but as days and then weeks passed they began to question what lay ahead. They had no maps or charts to help them since no Europeans had sailed here before.

Magellan's voyage, from the tip of South America to the Philippines, November 1520 to March 1521. In January 1521 they sighted land, but could not find any shallow water in which to anchor.

Guam

Philippines

Disappointment Island

In January 1521, the crew sighted land, but there was no harbor, and they could not drop anchor. They named it "Disappointment Island."

LIFE ABOARD THE VITTORIA

Many sailors fell ill with scurvy—a deadly disease caused by lack of vitamin C. Magellan stayed fit and well, probably because of his private supply of quince marmalade, made from vitamin-rich fruit.

Scurvy was a miserable disease. Sailors' gums bled, their teeth fell out, their joints swelled and ached, and their bodies became covered in sores. On the voyage across the Pacific, 20 members of Magellan's crew died of scurvy. Today we know that eating lots of fruit prevents scurvy.

Cebu

On March 16, they found safe anchorage in sheltered waters off the island of Cebu. Friendly local people gave Magellan and his crew palm oil, bananas, coconuts, and fish. The sailors ate and rested to build up their strength.

MURDER

Magellan and his crew were treated very kindly in the Philippines. Magellan and the King of Cebu gave each other gifts and became friends. Magellan learned that the King of Cebu had quarreled with a nearby ruler, and that Cebu soldiers were preparing to fight. To repay his host's hospitality, Magellan promised to help the king fight his enemies on the neighboring island of Mactan. He felt sure his guns and swords would defeat the Mactan's spears.

Philippines

Spreading the Gospel
Magellan converted the king to Christianity and, in a splendid ceremony, 800 islanders were baptised as Christians, too.

Gifts

In return for their kindness, food, and shelter, Magellan gave the Cebu islanders gifts of bells, mirrors, and lengths of brightly-colored cloth.

Magellan re-named Cebu and the neighboring islands "the Philippines," in honor of Crown Prince Philip, son of the King of Spain.

THE DEATH OF MAGELLAN

But, tragically, Magellan was wrong. Along with 40 of his men, he was stabbed to death in the battle against the Mactan islanders. Magellan and some of his crew were trapped ashore by Mactan warriors. Bravely, Magellan told his men to leave him, and to save their own lives. He was mourned by his men as a "brave and noble captain." Magellan's unexpected death left the crew in a state of shock.

Among them was the Portuguese Juan Lopes Carvalho, who took command. He was an experienced ships' pilot. Carvalho was jealous of Magellan's success and wanted to claim credit for the voyage himself. He reportedly destroyed Magellan's log-book to try to hide his achievements.

Pirates

Another of Magellan's ships, the *Concepcion*, was lost. Only the *Trinidad* and the *Vittoria* survived, along with about 108 of the original crew. Led by Carvalho, the crew spent two months as pirates. They robbed villagers and captured local sailors to help sail their ships.

19

SPICE ISLANDS

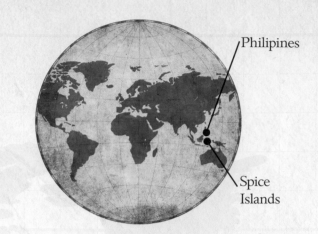

Philipines

Spice
Islands

Magellan was dead, but his voyage around South America and across the Pacific had established that it was possible to reach the Far East by sailing west. Now, in summer 1521, the surviving members of the crew decided to sail south from the Philippines to the rich Spice Islands. They wanted to load their ships with valuable spices before sailing home. After the fight on Mactan, they no longer felt friendly toward the local people. So they kidnapped some of them, and forced them to sail with them to show them the way.

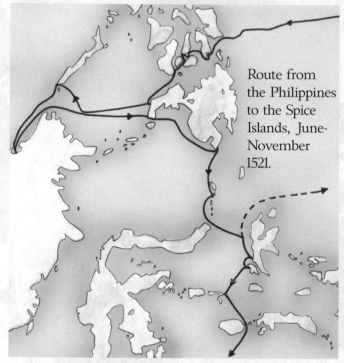

Route from the Philippines to the Spice Islands, June-November 1521.

Arriving

By November, the *Trinidad* and the *Vittoria* had reached the Spice Islands laden with pirated loot. The Sultan of Ternate sent his royal barge out to inspect the newly-arrived ships. He was suspicious of these ragged sailors, but allowed them to trade. Local sailors and traders hurried to meet them in outrigger canoes.

A FORTUNE TO BE MADE

The Spice Islands produced the world's best nutmeg, cloves, and mace. The crew bought these valuable spices along with silks, pearls, and tropical birds to sell when they got home. However, their good fortune came to a halt as sickness spread through the crews.

Fever

In the Spice Islands, Carvalho and many other members of the crew died of fever. Juan Sebastian del Cano, an experienced sailor from the Basque country in northern Spain, took command of the *Vittoria*.

The crowded harbor of Ternate was one of the busiest trading ports in the Spice Islands.

Going Home

In December 1521, del Cano decided to return to Europe in the *Vittoria*. The *Trinidad* stayed behind for urgent repairs. When the *Trinidad* was finally repaired it set out across the Pacific Ocean. Both ships had long, difficult, and very dangerous voyages home.

SAILING HOME

The *Vittoria* began its long journey home in December 1521, sailing westward around the tip of Africa. It was 28 months since it had set sail from Spain and though the return journey was shorter, it was just as hazardous. Del Cano, the senior surviving captain, planned the *Vittoria*'s homeward voyage. On board were 47 sailors from Magellan's original crew, plus 13 sailors recruited from the Spice Islands.

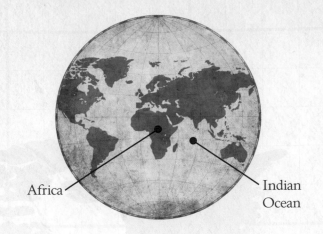

Africa   Indian Ocean

It took the *Vittoria* over two months to cross the Indian Ocean. In February 1522, the east African coast was sighted. But they dared not land, in case they met Portuguese soldiers.

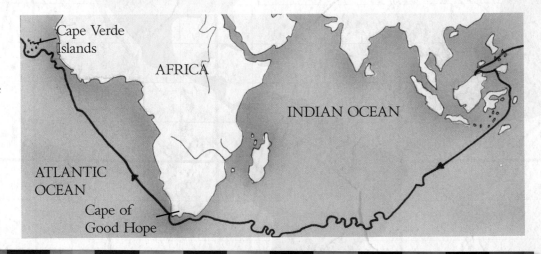

The *Vittoria*'s route home from the Spice Islands to Europe, December 1521-September 1522.

Cape Verde Islands

AFRICA

INDIAN OCEAN

ATLANTIC OCEAN

Cape of Good Hope

Mistakes

Del Cano was not as good a navigator as Magellan had been, and he often made mistakes. One such mistake at the Cape of Good Hope (at the tip of South Africa) added days to the voyage.

THE STRUGGLE TO RETURN

At the Cape, del Cano steered too far south. The *Vittoria* was buffeted by fierce gales and mountainous waves, and was almost wrecked by icebergs. In the wild South Atlantic Ocean, the crew often saw huge whales, and flying fish that followed the ship.

Desperate for food, the *Vittoria* anchored briefly in a sheltered bay on the West African coast early in May 1522. But the sailors were sick and tired, and scared of being attacked by local people.

Captured

On June 8 the *Vittoria* crossed the Equator. Most of the crew were ill and 15 men had died already. By July 9 the crew had run out of food. The ship had to land at the Cape Verde Islands, even though these islands belonged to the Portuguese. The sailors traded spices for fruit and rice. The Portuguese sent soldiers to arrest the crew of the *Vittoria*. Thirteen of them were captured and marched off to prison. On its homeward journey, the *Trinidad* lost many of its crew to scurvy. Others were imprisoned by the Portuguese. Only four of the crew escaped to Spain.

HOME AT LAST

In August 1522, the *Vittoria* sailed past the Azores—a group of islands in the Atlantic Ocean. But the *Vittoria* was beginning to leak. Would it survive the journey? The ship finally turned inland from the sea and sailed up the River Guadalquivir toward the port of Seville in Spain.

On September 8, 1522, the dockers and sailors on Seville's quayside looked on aghast at the battered ship. The *Vittoria* and its sailors had been gone so long, it seemed they were returning from the dead.

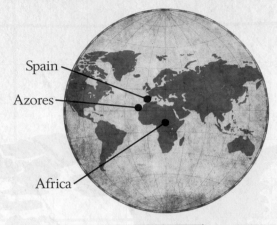

Spain
Azores
Africa

The last stage of the journey home, August-September 1522.

Seville

Azores

AFRICA

Astonishment!

The citizens of Seville were astonished to see the *Vittoria* sail into the harbor. Most people believed that the ship had sunk many months ago. Once the people of Seville had got over their shock and surprise, del Cano and the survivors were given a heroes' welcome.

FIRST VOYAGE AROUND THE WORLD

On September 9, the day after the sailors arrived home in Seville, they walked in a solemn, barefoot procession through the city streets to the church of Santa Maria de la Vittoria. They lit candles in front of the church altar, and said prayers to thank God for their safe journey home. They knew they were very lucky to be alive. Only 17 members of Magellan's original crew of 270 men had survived.

The *Vittoria* sails into Seville harbor at last.

A Royal Welcome

King Charles of Spain invited del Cano and all the crew to his royal palace to congratulate them. When the *Vittoria*'s cargo was sold, it only raised enough money to cover the original costs of fitting out Magellan's five ships.

DEL CANO

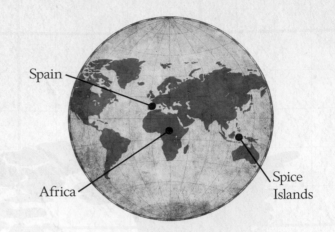

The *Vittoria*'s record-breaking voyage was Magellan's idea and would not have happened without his courage and determination. Yet few people recognized Magellan's courage during the voyage, or even remembered his heroic death. Del Cano took all the credit for sailing the *Vittoria* around the world, and blamed Magellan for everything that had gone wrong with the voyage. But in 1529, King Charles proclaimed that Magellan was not to blame.

Today, we remember Magellan, del Cano, and the sailors on the *Vittoria* for a great achievement— the first voyage around the world.

What's more, Magellan and del Cano proved beyond all doubt that the earth was round. Soon, geographers and craftworkers began to make globes like this.

Trade Winds

Trade winds blow in a regular pattern across the Pacific Ocean, in one direction only. These winds aided Magellan's outward journey, but the ships had to battle against the wind to return across the Pacific.

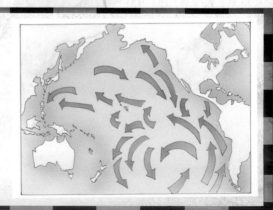

OTHER VOYAGES

The *Vittoria*'s success inspired other explorers to plan new voyages. They hoped to make their fortunes by trading with the rich Spice Islands.

The next successful voyage around the world did not take place for more than 50 years.

In 1577, the English explorer Francis Drake set sail from Plymouth. Drake also sailed westward across the Atlantic and the Pacific, then around southern Africa. His ship, the Golden Hind, finally returned home in 1580.

Del Cano's Fate

In 1525, del Cano hoped to circumnavigate the world again. This was a brave decision, after the hardships and dangers of his first trip. Like many of the sailors on his earlier voyage, del Cano died of disease while crossing the Pacific Ocean. He was buried at sea that year.

In the short term, Magellan's voyage round the world had been a disaster, and it had failed to make a profit. But Magellan's murder, the deaths among the crew, and the *Vittoria*'s three year voyage made one thing clear. The westward journey to the Spice Islands was much longer and much more dangerous than the better-known eastward voyage around the tip of Africa and across the Indian Ocean.

The discovery of the trade winds discouraged others from copying Magellan's voyage. They realized that if they headed westward from Europe to the Spice Islands they could not turn back but would have to sail right around the world. After Magellan's and del Cano's experiences on board the *Vittoria*, that was not an inviting prospect! The Pacific Ocean's dangerous reputation increased after 1525 when del Cano died there, trying to make a second exploration of the Pacific.

WHAT HAPPENED NEXT?

It was not until 1565 that a Spanish sailor, Urdaneta, discovered a way of crossing the Pacific from Asia to America that avoided the trade winds. He sailed far north from the Spice Islands then headed for the west coast of America, skirting round the vast expanse of ocean where the trade winds blew. But it was still a long, dangerous voyage. Throughout the 16th century, adventurers, explorers, and map makers concentrated on investigating North and South America. It was not until 1577 that Englishman Francis Drake dared to set off on another round-the-world voyage.

Both Spain and Portugal wanted to prove that the Spice Islands belonged to them. But inaccurate 16th-century methods of measuring latitude at sea made it impossible to solve the dispute. Sailors were not able to measure latitude accurately for more than 200 years, until English clockmaker John Harrington invented a chronometer—a very accurate timekeeper—in 1759. However, in 1527, King Charles V of Spain agreed to give up Spain's claim in return for a payment from Portugal of 350,000 solid gold coins. Charles made this agreement because he was running short of money to finance a war with France.

There were political disappointments, too, as a result of the *Vittoria*'s voyage. For years the rulers of Spain and Portugal had been quarreling over who had the right to claim the lands visited by Spanish and Portuguese explorers. They made an agreement in 1494, in the Treaty of Tordesillas, but, secretly, both sides hoped to claim extra lands.

In the long term, Magellan and del Cano's round-the-world voyage was a success. It showed both men's courage and daring. It also proved, once and for all, that the world was round.

GLOSSARY

Caravans
Herds of specially-trained camels, used to carry heavy loads for long distances over dry or desert land.

Carracks
Huge, slow-moving ships with big square sails. They were designed to carry large loads of valuable cargo in their wide, deep hulls. Merchants from Spain and Portugal sailed in carracks to trade with the Spice Islands and, later, the New World.

Circumnavigation
A round-the-world voyage.

Latitude
Position north or south of the Equator—an imaginary line drawn around the widest part of the Earth.

Mace
A valuable spice grown only in tropical lands. Mace is the name given to the outer coating of nutmeg (see below). It has a slightly sweet, peppery flavor.

Mutiny
A rebellion by soldiers or sailors against the officers who command them.

Nutmeg
A valuable spice produced by trees growing in hot, moist climates. It has a warm, spicy flavor.

Porcelain
Very fine, white pottery made from a special kind of clay. In Magellan's time it was only produced in China.

Scurvy
A serious disease caused by lack of vitamin C. It killed many sailors in Magellan's time. It can be prevented by eating fresh fruit and vegetables.

Spice Islands
A group of islands in present-day Indonesia. Because of their year-round hot weather and plentiful rainfall, the world's best-quality spices were produced there.

Strait
A narrow channel where the sea runs between two land masses.

Trade winds
Winds that blow in one direction only for most of the year. The name "trade" comes from the word "trodden". People in the past said that the winds "trod" the same path.

INDEX